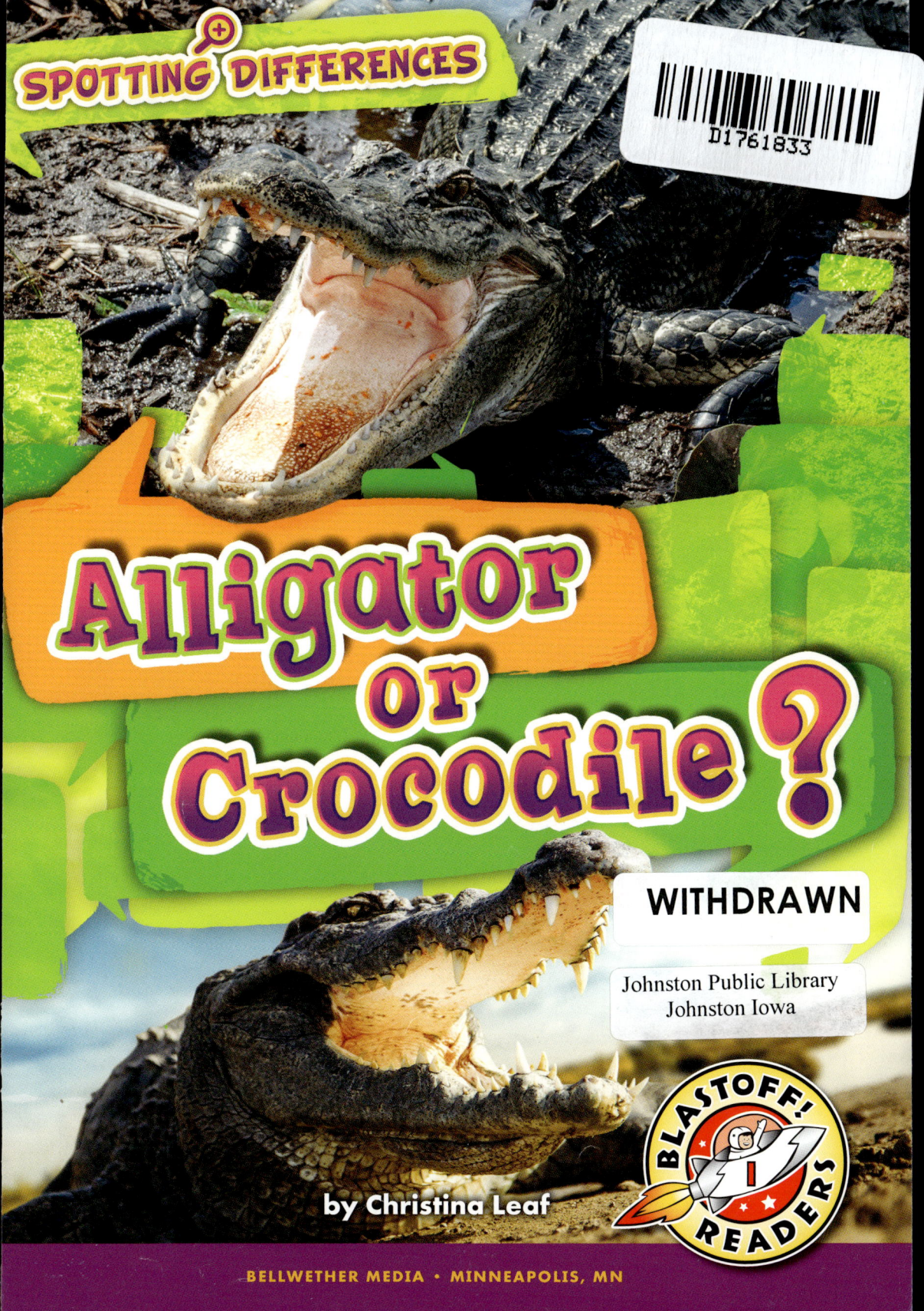

Note to Librarians, Teachers, and Parents:

Blastoff! Readers are carefully developed by literacy experts and combine standards-based content with developmentally appropriate text.

Level 1 provides the most support through repetition of high-frequency words, light text, predictable sentence patterns, and strong visual support.

Level 2 offers early readers a bit more challenge through varied simple sentences, increased text load, and less repetition of high-frequency words.

Level 3 advances early-fluent readers toward fluency through increased text and concept load, less reliance on visuals, longer sentences, and more literary language.

Level 4 builds reading stamina by providing more text per page, increased use of punctuation, greater variation in sentence patterns, and increasingly challenging vocabulary.

Level 5 encourages children to move from "learning to read" to "reading to learn" by providing even more text, varied writing styles, and less familiar topics.

Whichever book is right for your reader, Blastoff! Readers are the perfect books to build confidence and encourage a love of reading that will last a lifetime!

This edition first published in 2020 by Bellwether Media, Inc.

No part of this publication may be reproduced in whole or in part without written permission of the publisher. For information regarding permission, write to Bellwether Media, Inc., Attention: Permissions Department, 6012 Blue Circle Drive, Minnetonka, MN 55343.

Library of Congress Cataloging-in-Publication Data

Names: Leaf, Christina, author.
Title: Alligator or Crocodile? / by Christina Leaf.
Description: Minneapolis, MN : Bellwether Media, Inc., [2020] | Series: Blastoff! Readers: Spotting Differences | Audience: Age 5-8. | Audience: K to Grade 3. | Includes bibliographical references and index.
Identifiers: LCCN 2018054606 (print) | LCCN 2018056486 (ebook) | ISBN 9781618915719 (ebook) | ISBN 9781644870303 (hardcover : alk. paper)
Subjects: LCSH: Alligators--Juvenile literature. | Crocodiles--Juvenile literature.
Classification: LCC QL666.C925 (ebook) | LCC QL666.C925 L43 2020 (print) | DDC 597.98/4--dc23
LC record available at https://lccn.loc.gov/2018054606

Text copyright © 2020 by Bellwether Media, Inc. BLASTOFF! READERS and associated logos are trademarks and/or registered trademarks of Bellwether Media, Inc. SCHOLASTIC, CHILDREN'S PRESS, and associated logos are trademarks and/or registered trademarks of Scholastic Inc., 557 Broadway, New York, NY 10012.

Editor: Al Albertson   Designer: Jeffrey Kollock

Printed in the United States of America, North Mankato, MN.

Table of Contents

Alligators and Crocodiles	4
Different Looks	8
Different Lives	16
Side by Side	20
Glossary	22
To Learn More	23
Index	24

Alligators and Crocodiles

Alligators and crocodiles are big **reptiles**! They live near water.

alligator

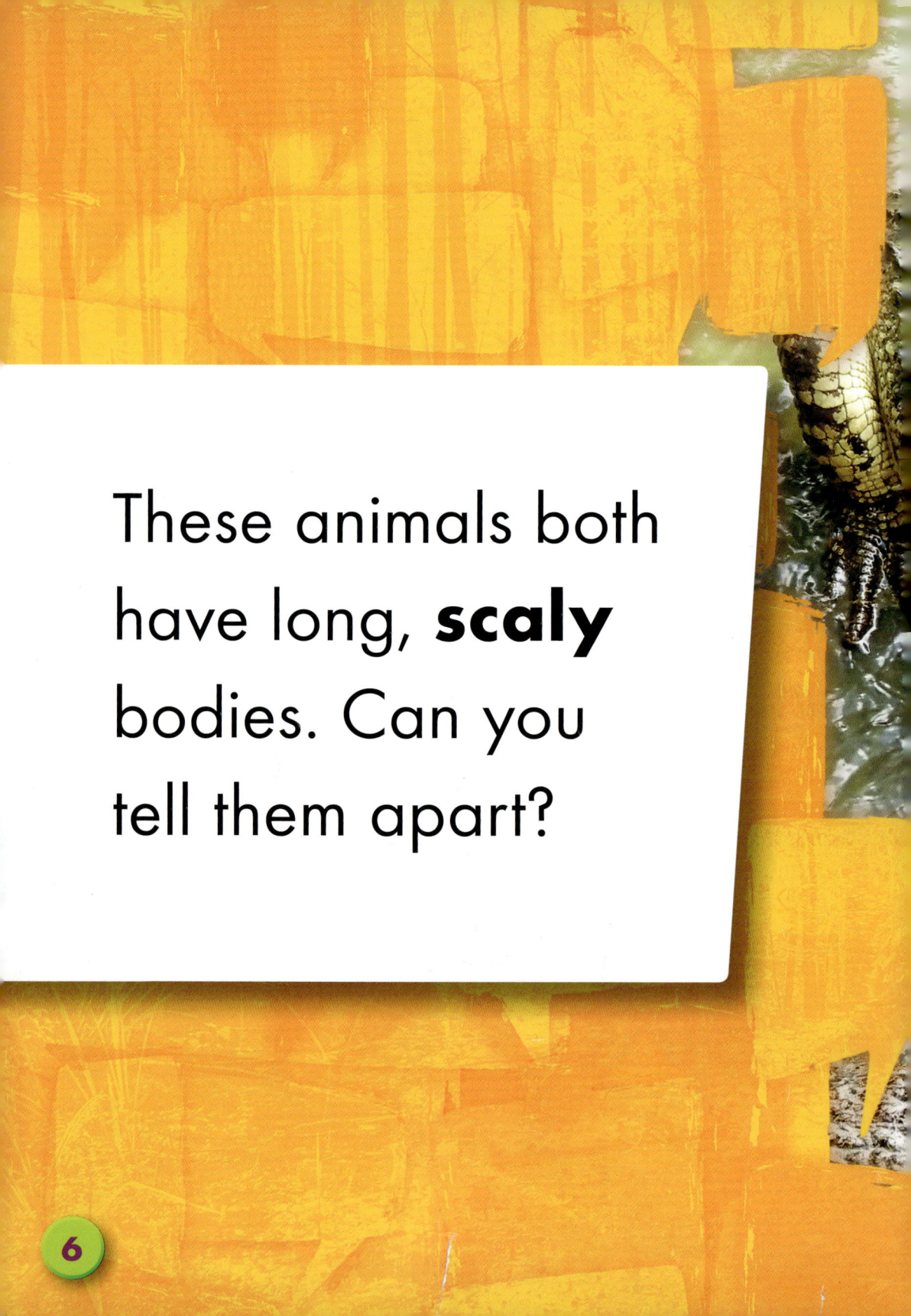

These animals both have long, **scaly** bodies. Can you tell them apart?

Different Looks

Snout shapes give clues. Alligator snouts look like a U. Crocodile snouts are pointed like a V!

V-shaped snout

U-shaped snout

Crocodiles have toothy grins. Their teeth always show. Alligators close their mouths to hide their bottom teeth.

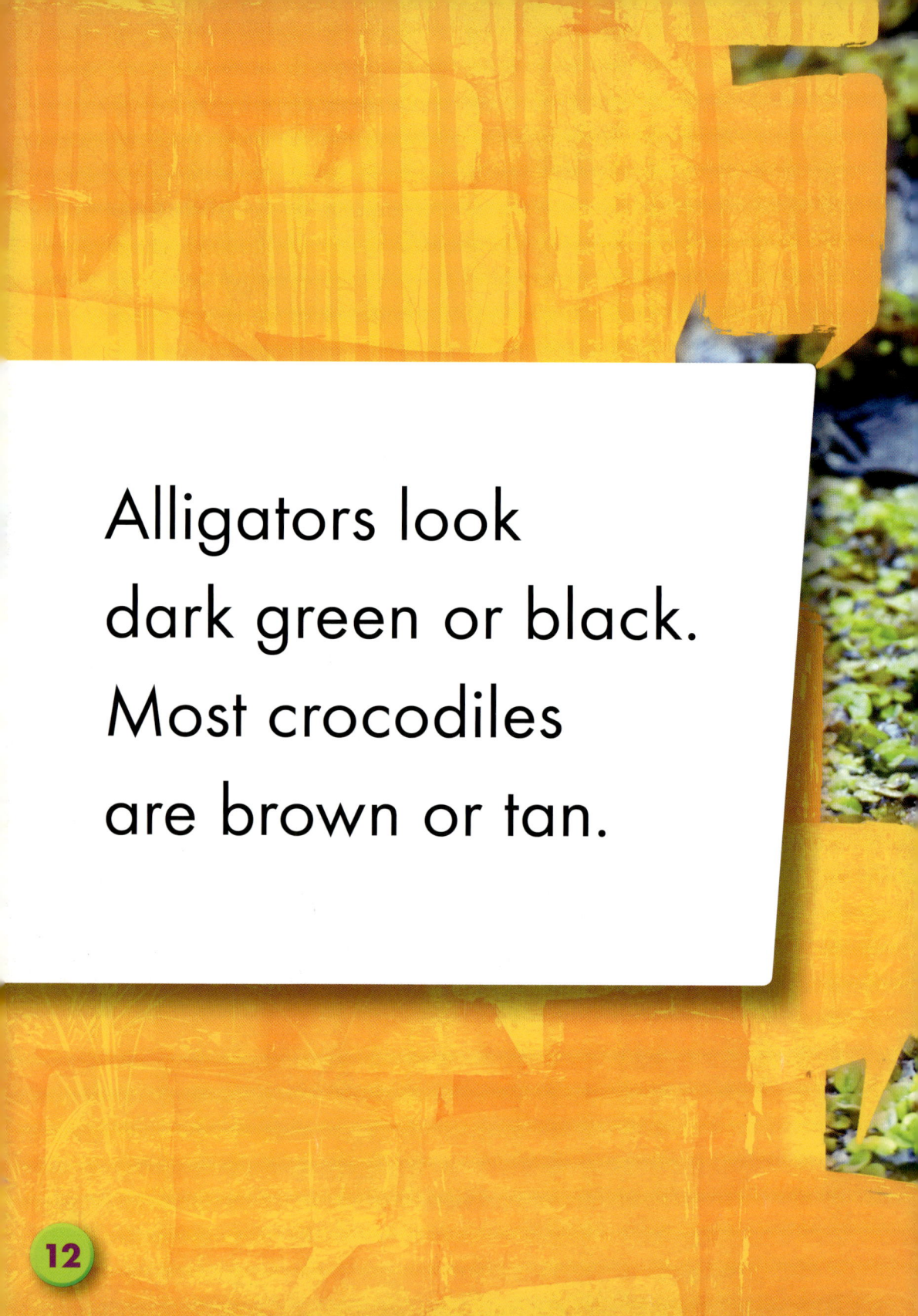

Alligators look dark green or black. Most crocodiles are brown or tan.

Crocodiles are the larger animals. Some grow up to 23 feet (7 meters) long!

Different Lives

Crocodiles live around the world. Alligators make homes in two countries.

Alligators like **freshwater**. Crocodiles can swim in salty seawater. Which swimmer is this?

Side by Side

smaller size

U-shaped snout

black or green color

no bottom teeth showing

Alligator Differences

live near freshwater

live in China and the United States

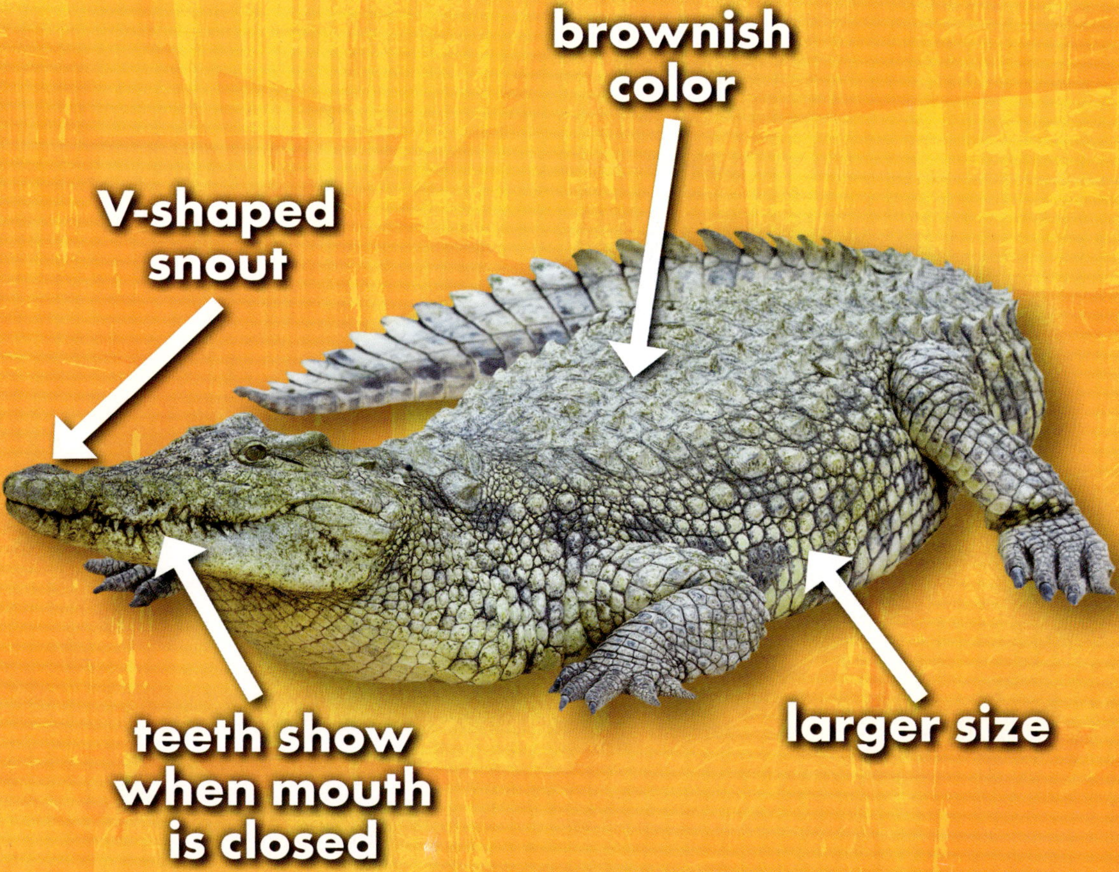

brownish color

V-shaped snout

teeth show when mouth is closed

larger size

Crocodile Differences

can swim in saltwater

live across the world

21

Glossary

freshwater

water that is not salty; freshwater fills rivers, lakes, and ponds.

scaly

covered in bony plates called scales

reptiles

cold-blooded animals that have bony plates or scales and breathe air

snout

the nose of an animal

To Learn More

AT THE LIBRARY
Black, Vanessa. *Alligators*. Minneapolis, Minn.: Bullfrog Books, 2017.

Hansen, Grace. *Saltwater Crocodiles*. Minneapolis, Minn.: Abdo Kids Jumbo, 2019.

Marsh, Laura. *Alligators and Crocodiles*. Washington, D.C.: National Geographic Society, 2015.

ON THE WEB

FACTSURFER

Factsurfer.com gives you a safe, fun way to find more information.

1. Go to www.factsurfer.com.

2. Enter "alligator or crocodile" into the search box and click 🔍.

3. Select your book cover to see a list of related web sites.

Index

animals, 6, 14
bodies, 6
countries, 16
freshwater, 18
grins, 10
grow, 14
homes, 16
mouths, 10
reptiles, 4
scales, 7
seawater, 18
snout, 8, 9
swim, 18

teeth, 10
water, 4

The images in this book are reproduced through the courtesy of: Brittany Mason, front cover (alligator); StanislavBeloglazov, front cover (crocodile); Heiko Kiera, pp. 4-5; 168 STUDIO, pp. 6-7; apple2499, p. 7 (scales); mark stephens photography, pp. 8-9; David Havel, p. 9 (v-shaped snout); Meister Photo, pp. 10-11; Pbd1950, p. 11 (bubble); Don Mammoser, pp. 12-13; Robby Holmwood, pp. 14-15; Alexandra Machulskiy, pp. 16-17; christopher smith, Alamy, pp. 18-19; reptiles4all, p. 20 (alligator); Kichigin, p. 20 (freshwater); ATGImages, p. 20 (bubble); Lefteris Papaulakis, p. 21 (crocodile); Allexxandar, p. 21 (saltwater); Damsea, p. 22 (freshwater); Dan Goro, p. 22 (reptile); Patrick Rolands, p. 22 (scaly); Arto Hakola, p. 22 (snout).